Gwathmey & Siegel

ROCKPORT

Gwathmey & Siegel

ROCKPORT PUBLISHERS

GLOUCESTER MASSACHUSETTS

Editor: Sofía Cheviakoff

Texts: Gwathmey & Siegel

Graphic Design: Emma Termes Parera

Layout: Soti Mas-Bagà

Translation of the captions: William Bain

Library of Congress Cataloging-in-Publication Data available

ISBN: 1-56496-984-3

10 9 8 7 6 5 4 3 2 1

Printed in China

Founded in 1968, this firm of architects with its headquarters in New York offers services in architecture, town planning, interior decoration, and the design of objects. In the course of its 32 years in professional practice, the company has developed more than three hundred projects in different parts of the world. Among these are projects of a corporate, educational, cultural, governmental, and private character.

The more than 80 people that comprise the group have earned an international reputation with some 100 design awards, a continuous renown in both the general and the specialized presses, and inclusion of their works in numerous exhibitions and books on contemporary architecture.

In 1982, Gwathmey & Siegel was the first office of young architects to receive the highest honor of the American Institute of Architects (AIA): the award for planning each project with a fresh look, meticulous attention to details, a sensitive appreciation of the environmental and economic factors… and for "their unshakeable confidence in the efforts of collaboration."

The firm is widely known for proposals that take in everything from the smallest design detail in interiors to the aspects related to the site and its environment.

Charles Gwathmey and Robert Seigel are responsible for the area of design, although they also actively participate in the development of each project, the area of their architectural associates.

The 12 associates are architects who have been a part of the team for periods that range between 12 and 25 years. They supervise the teams designated to oversee each project. They are additionally responsible for the selection and coordination of engineers and specialized consultants and act as a link between the firm and its clients.

The clients themselves actively participate in giving form to the programs and determining the directions of the designs. The interest of these professionals is to develop the project on the basis of interaction and analysis. The teams are sensitive to the nuanced interplay between the site and its conditioners. A large part of their work consists of projects for campuses and city centers, as well as in extension and refurbishing work with historic buildings.

Gwathmey & Siegel's renovation of and addition to the Solomon R. Guggenheim Museum in New York City is one of the firm's most celebrated and critically acclaimed works. It contains 51,000 square feet of new and renovated gallery space, 15,000 square feet of new office space, a restored theater, a new restaurant and retrofitted support and storage spaces.

Both Wright's proposed annex of 1949-52, and William Wesley Peters' annex, originally designed as a ten-story structure, are acknowledged by the new addition. Its part was determined by two critical intersections with the original building, first, with the rotunda at the existing circulation core, and second, with the monitor building along its east wall. It provides balcony views and access to the rotunda from three new two-story galleries and one single-story gallery. A transparent glass wall, connecting the monitor building and the addition, reveals the original facades from both the outside-in and the inside-out.

The pavilions are now integrated functionally and spatially with the large rotunda as well as with the new addition. The new fifth-floor roof sculpture terrace, the large rotunda roof terrace, and the renovated public ramp reveal the original building in a new extended and comprehensive perspective.

The entire original structure is now devoted to exhibition space. Each ramp cycle affords the option of entry or views to new galleries. Within the rotunda, numerous technical refinements have corrected omissions in the original construction and brought the building up to current museum standards. Re-glazing the central lantern, opening the clerestories between the turns of the spiral wall, and restoring the scalloped flat clerestory at the perimeter of the ground floor exhibition space have recaptured the sensitivity to light evident in Wright's original design.

Collaborators: Severud Associates (Structural Engineers)
John L. Altieri Consulting Engineers (MEP Engineers)
Light and Space Associates LTD (Lighting Designers)
George A. Fuller Col (General Contractor)
Lehrer McGovern Bovis

Location: New York, USA
Area: 15,000 sq. ft.
Construction Date: 1992
Photography: Jeff Goldberg/Esto

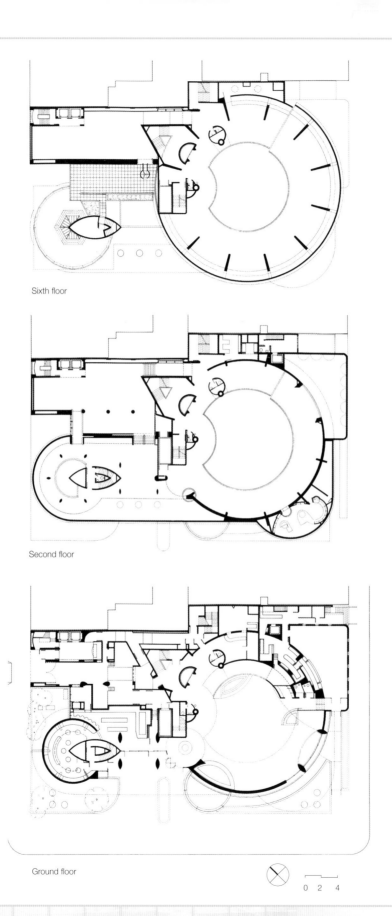

Sixth floor

Second floor

Ground floor

0 2 4

Substituting the glass panes of the central skylight and modernizing the public access ramp are two of the tasks involved in the renovation of this emblematic building.

Some of the new galleries are double height and maintain a visual link with the main traffic route.

The Fifth Avenue façade

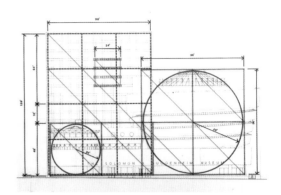

System of proportions based on the golden mean

0 2 4

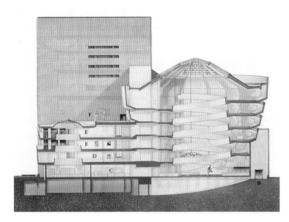

Section through the rotunda

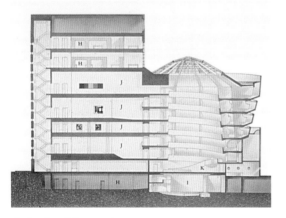

Section through the rear volume

0 2 4

At ground level, the entry separates the garage and service areas from the children's bedrooms, and allows direct access to the pool terrace.

A circulation zone runs parallel to the two story exterior glazed wall, connecting both full and half levels of the house physically and visually. A ramp leads from the entry to the first half level where it is terminated by the master bedroom. There a spiral stair leads to a sleeping loft, oriented towards the ocean, and overlooking the sitting room below.

The second floor provides a loft-like sequence of living/dining/kitchen spaces open to views of the ocean.

Located below the existing grade at "basement" level is the screening room, exercise room, service and mechanical areas. This below-grade level becomes a plinth for the remainder of the house.

The extensive program of this house was resolved into one coherent composition by interlocking building volumes with outdoor spaces within the framework of the site. This resulted in inventive sectional and circulation manipulations.

This private residence is located on a three-acre site defined by the Pacific Coast Highway to the north, the Pacific Ocean to the south and existing two story residences to the east and west. The intention of the design was to create the perception of an expansive site, as well as to maximize the size of the building to accommodate an extensive program.

The program requirements included a main house and garage, swimming pool, guest house, and tennis court. The planning strategy was to integrate building, outdoor spaces and landscape through interlocking volumes, resulting in an ordered sequence of layers in both the north-south and east-west axes. The tree-lined entry drive along the western edge of the site screens the guest house and tennis court to the east. The drive ends in a landscaped autocourt, which acts as a transition between the guest house/lawn area and the main house and pool area, located at the southern edge of the site parallel to the bluff and ocean.

Location: Malibu, California, USA
Construction Date: 1999
Area: 10,000 sq. ft.
Photography: Edhard Pfeiffer

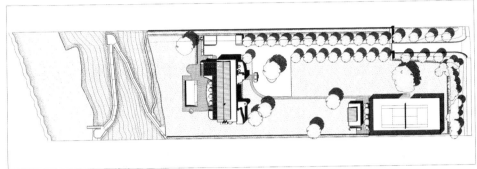

Situation plan

0   3   6

The exterior spaces link with the interior and intermediate ones so that the house establishes a dialogue with the site on which it has been raised. The northwest façade opens onto the garden, which has a swimming pool. This façade uses oversized windows and terraces, while the southwest front is clearly more closed, and oriented toward the access road.

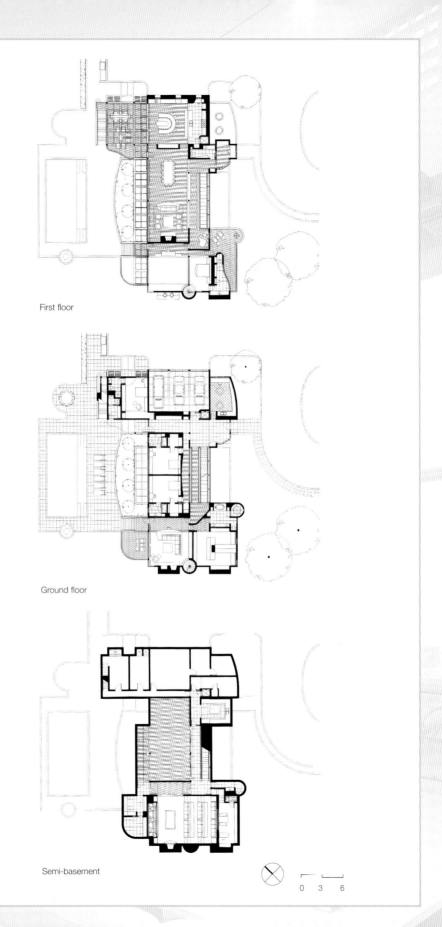

First floor

Ground floor

Semi-basement

0 3 6

The louver regulates the entrance of light through the large window running the length of the house. This aperture establishes a strict visual relationship among all of the spaces in the dwelling and with the garden.

The four-story, 135,000-square-foot building extends between the one-story architecture and engineering buildings, its length interrupted by a grand three-story portal that acts as the school's formal entrance and leads to the campus quadrangle. The building materials are white ceramic tile, aluminum, corrugated panels, and zinc shingles.

The initial analysis of the building site also resulted in a complete transformation of the campus plan. Formerly, the main road continued through the middle of the central quadrangle, impeding pedestrian flow among the main academic buildings.

Collaborators: Neumann/Smith & Associates
Location: Southfield, Michigan, USA
Area: 135,000 sq. ft.
Construction Date: 2001
Photography: Justin Maconochie

With the introduction of the Technology and Learning Complex, the road now circles the campus perimeter, with parking relocated to the edge. The result is a pedestrian quadrangle, with the Technology and Learning Complex completing its architectural frame. A new landscape plan features tree-lined paths connecting the buildings that border it.

The University Technology and Learning Complex, which is now under construction, will be the new formal gateway building to Lawrence Technological University and the centerpiece of its campus. It will provide campus-wide services, updating and expanding those of current teaching facilities with state-of-the-art classrooms, learning laboratories and facilities for long distance learning. The project has also resulted in a redesign of the central campus as a pedestrian-focused quadrangle.

The complex offers comprehensive facilities for learning in an electronic environment with fully wired classrooms, a virtual reality lab, an advanced graphic lab, a lighting lab, electrical engineering and computer labs, a photography studio, and TV production and broadcasting studio space. It also offers a major exhibition and lecture room, an office of the future, a resource center with a 15,000-volume library, conference rooms, and office spaces. The ground floor lobby announces the building's focus on technology with an information commons that offers computer stations available for campus information, group teaching, and individual research.

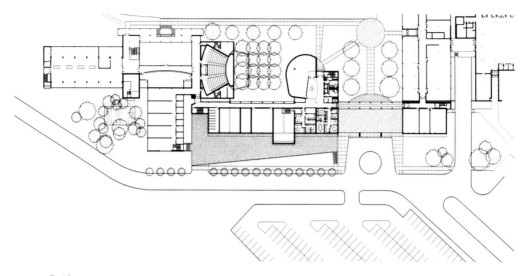

First floor

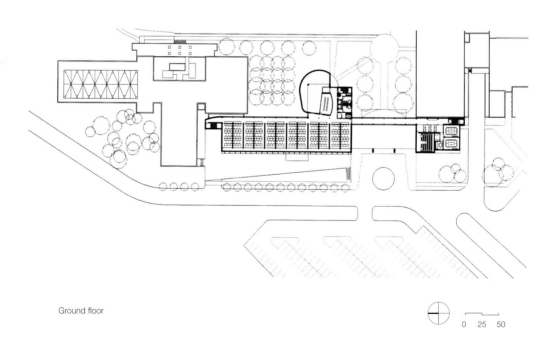

Ground floor

0   25   50

The body configuring the campus entrance is a double-height façade faced in corrugated zinc panels. It is presided over by a low portico containing two galleries that link both sides of the building.

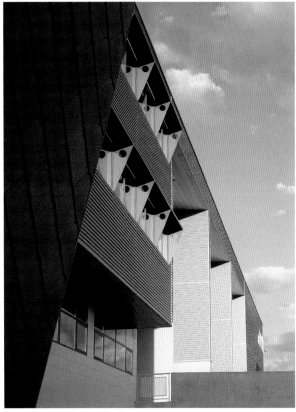

Designed as an undergraduate teaching facility, this 42,000 square-foot physics building links the Physics Department's graduate research facility with the Mathematics Department, creating a courtyard plaza that recalls the traditional quadrangle layout of the older areas of campus.

Three major programmatic divisions—lecture halls, classrooms and labs—are articulated by both their massing and materials as discrete segments.

Located partially underground, two lecture halls form a base for two volumes: a cast stone element consisting of five classrooms and service areas faces the plaza; a zinc-clad element (rotated to resolve the varying geometries of adjoining buildings) contains five labs and a lab prep room and provides frontal orientation toward the main circulation path. The public circulation acts as a wrapper unifying the three volumes.

A canopy marks the entrance to a double-height atrium, which connects the new building to Jadwin Hall and provides access to five classrooms, two labs, and a prep room. The barrel-vaulted ceilings of three additional labs allow tall experimental set-ups involving gravity and motion studies. An exterior stair leads down to a second entrance, where the original gallery was refurbished to create lobby space for two new lecture halls. The halls are steeply raked and provided with rear projection facilities, catwalks, and turntable stages, which allow large-scale experiments to be set up in the prep room behind the stage and then rotated into the lecture halls. All three buildings are linked, allowing multiple access to the lecture halls.

Collaborators: Severud Associates (Structures)
Location: Princeton, New Jersey, USA
Area: 42,000 sq. ft.
Construction Date: 1998
Photography: Norman McGrath

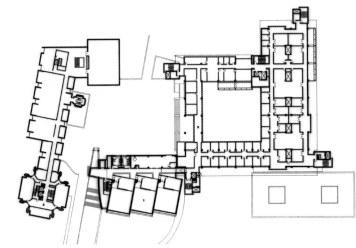

Second floor

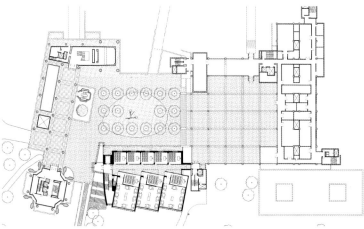

Ground floor

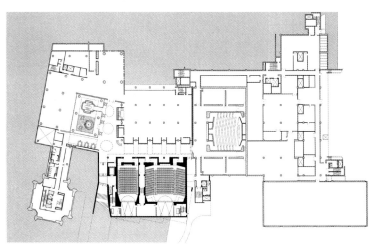

Semi-basement

0 25 50

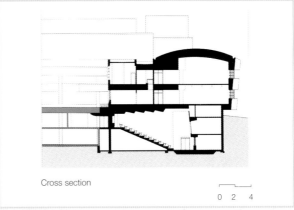

Cross section

0 2 4

The building is made up of two bodies faced in different materials, stone and metal. The lower section is partially subgrade and serves as base for the other section.

On the second floor, a corridor connects the five west-facing laboratories with three additional labs whose high ceilings were designed to allow the setting up of experiments requiring height. On the ground floor, a large vestibule that also interfaces with the adjacent buildings makes up the anteroom of the two large conference halls.

The conference rooms, which are on the ground floor, are on a considerable incline so as to guarantee good acoustics and audience visibility. They also have a large projection control panel worked from a room at the back as well as a revolving stage that makes it possible to set up two experiments simultaneously.

This fifty-two-story office tower houses the world head-quarters of the international investment banking firm, Morgan Stanley Dean Witter and Co. Located in mid-town Manhattan, the building reflects the aspirations of a traditional skyscraper to present an appropriately scaled public building at the pedestrian base and a strong silhouette on the skyline.

One of the challenges presented by the program involved the site's unusual shape and positioning, which the architects resolved by generating forms that address both the diagonal of Broadway and the orthog-onal Manhattan street grid. The base responds to the diagonal; the segmented curve of the double-height mechanical floor creates a transition from the rotated base to the orthogonal tower. The changing play of nat-ural light on the building's glass surface produces images of both opacity and reflectivity, of fluidity and permanence. Morgan Stanley Dean Witter's interior design includes executive offices, dining and meeting spaces, and boardrooms on the 40th and 41st floors, the main lobby on street level, and dining facilities for five hundred people on the lower level.

The executive floor entry space is rendered in granite, anaigre, mahogany, and ebonized cherry woods. Offering a panoramic view south, east, and west of Manhattan, the two-story entry acts as a referential interconnected volume for the executive floors. The selection of materials imbues the entire space with a sense of density, permanence, and inevitability. The public lobby is a sweeping expanse broken only by two columns. The walls are finished with gray granite accented by stripes of dark green polished marble. Other materials include white, black, and dark green marble in a geometric pattern on the floor, and a cof-fered ceiling of wood. An opening in the lobby floor accommodates new escalators, stairs, and an access bridge to a dining environment for five hundred.

Collaborators: Gensler and Associates
Architects (B2 building)
Emery Roth & Sins PC
(B3 building)
Location: 1585 Broadway, New York, USA
Area: 1,300,000 sq. ft.
Construction Date: 1990 (building),
1995 (interior)
Photography: Peter Aaron/Esto,
Jeff Goldberg/Esto

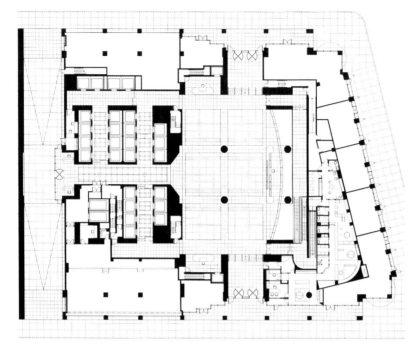

Ground level

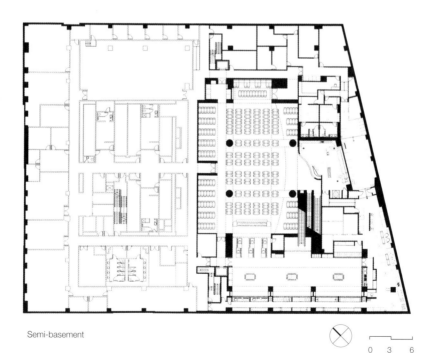

Semi-basement

0   3   6

In the dining area, entrance is through a walkway; the escalators and the service stairs join the grade level with the semi-basement.

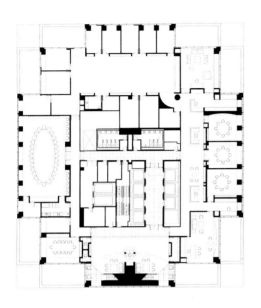

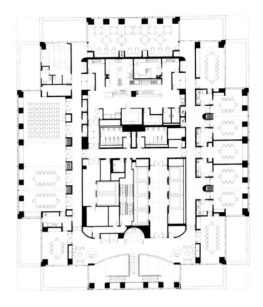

Typical ground plans

0 2 4

This private residence is located on one and a half acres in a quiet residential neighborhood at the end of Malibu Canyon. A bilateral part derived from the site's unique profile—the majesty, the quiet, the calm, the stillness, the shadows, and the density of Malibu Canyon in contrast with the sparkling, sun-drenched horizon of daytime and the equally bright city lights at night afforded an opportunity to design two distinctly different ideals and combine them into an architectural collage.

A three-story curved limestone pavilion housing the main living spaces is poised on a promontory looking south and east toward Santa Monica, the Pacific Ocean, and the skyline of downtown Los Angeles. A three-story cube containing support space is embedded in the slope behind, overlooking the canyon to the west.

In addition to the two house structures, there is a third element—the site-building. Creating the site—extending the two horizontal planes at different levels—involved constructing massive retaining walls (with caissons extending 65 feet to bedrock) and provided a unique opportunity for the site integration and building organization. If one removed the house from the land, the retaining walls would be a formally resolved composition, as well as a transformed ruin.

The "canyon house" was designed as a building in the ground, anchoring and stabilizing the pavilion, an object on the ground. Separate, unique, and contrapuntal in its organization and its materiality, the pavilion, with its curved limestone wall, could be read as a found object, an archeological fragment, transforming the experience of the landscape as one moves through it from the ordered programmatic distribution of the canyon house.

The canyon house is embedded in the ground and is organized vertically and bilaterally. Contained in the light-filled perimeter that overviews the canyon are the exercise room on the ground level, the children's bedrooms on the entry level, and an office/conference suite on the upper level.

Collaborators: Severud Associates (Structures),
Burton & Co. (Landscape)
Location: Pacific Palisades, California, USA
Construction Date: 1998
Area: 17,000 sq. ft.
Photography: Farshid Assassi

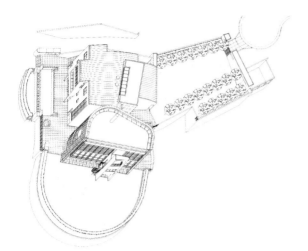

Axonometric perspective

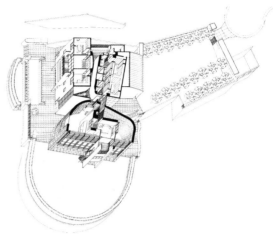

Axonometric perspective of the second floor

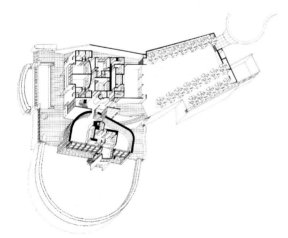

Axonometric perspective of the first floor

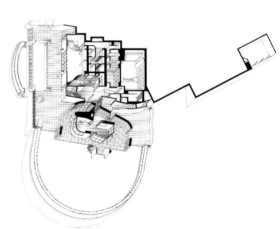

Axonometric perspective of the ground floor

0 2 4

The building is sited on the slope of two platforms. A third platform includes the street access. The two main bodies give onto the south and the west.

Each of the elements that form part of the interplay in the different volumes of the construction is of a different material. The successive zones are joined by slight changes in grade differentiating them from one another.

In the limestone pavilion, a large double-height space contains the dining room and the living room. The space is limited by a curved wall embracing it, and it looks onto the city panoramas and the ocean through an oversize window.

Renovation of a two-story, ground and lower level, 24,000 square foot space, in an existing office building, into a photography museum.

The ground floor contains the entry lobby, reception, museum store, and initial galleries.

The lower level, accessed through a double-height stair volume, contains galleries, café, and support space.

The space was designed to accommodate varying scales of exhibitions as well as to establish an optimum state-of-the-art museum environment.

The space has been transformed into an inspirational and memorable architectural sequence. It is simultaneously dense and open, simple and complex, with a clear objective to make the architecture as pertinent as the exhibitions it contains.

Collaborators: Severud Associates
(Structural Engineers)
Fisher Marantz Stone
(Lighting Consultant)
B&F Building Corporation
(Contractor)
Location: 1114 Avenue of Americas,
New York, USA
Area: 24,000 sq. ft.
Construction Date: 2001
Photography: Paul Warchol

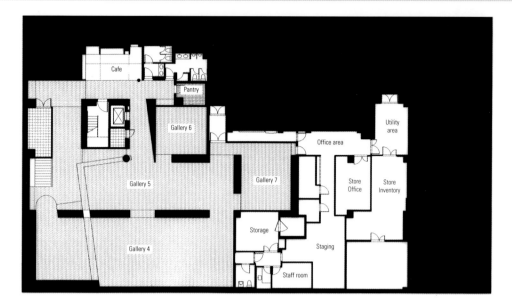

First floor

0   5   10 ft

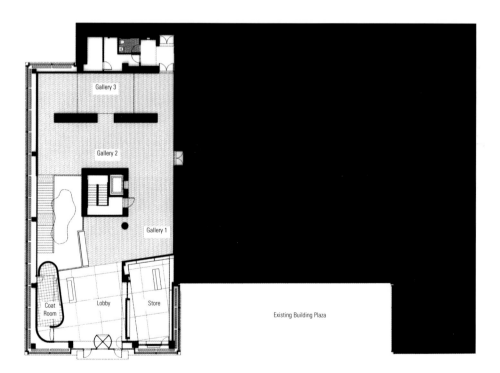

Ground floor

Gwathmey & Siegel's intention in the ICP renovation was to simultaneously integrate to counterpoint architecture and photography to evoke positive spiritual and perceptual responses. The presence of the new galleries is unique, both in their large scale and their architectural articulation.

The contextual challenges posed by the renovation of and addition to the Henry Art Gallery not only afforded the opportunity to recast the 1926 Carl F. Gould building as the primary element of the west campus entry to the University of Washington, but in fact propelled the design and helped to define the program.

A 10,000 square foot, two-story masonry structure, the original Henry was both overwhelmed by large neighboring buildings and compromised by an existing pedestrian bridge. Initially intended to be the north wing of a large, symmetrical arts complex that was never realized, the existing Henry now contains the permanent collection galleries, Reed Study Center, and curatorial offices. Gwathmey & Siegel's three-story addition offsets the original structure with textured stainless steel, cast-in-place concrete and cast-stone. It houses flexible, top-lighted galleries, administrative offices, and loading, storage and conservation spaces, as well as a new lobby, museum store, and lecture theater.

But perhaps most important, the intervention visually separates the museum and addition from adjacent structures, affording a legitimate transition, a new sense of place, an expectant and enriched entry sequence, and an integration of site, circulation, and context. In counterpoint to the original Henry, the new main gallery constitutes a memorable form to be re-experienced from within. The addition also acts as a carving away of a solid, revealing fragments that interact with the original Henry to re-site it as the asymmetrical—though primary—object in a new contextual frame, unifying the multiple architectural and site issues at the end of Campus Parkway.

Finally, the intervention is an architectural collage that unifies disparate elements in both contrapuntal and asymmetrical variations. The variations reestablish the primary site axis to Suzzallo Library, reconcile the vertical transition from the street to the plaza level, and integrate the original Henry façade both with the new sculpture court and gallery entry and with the campus entry. As fragments, the forms imply but do not directly reveal their spaces.

Collaborators: Loschky, Marquardt & Nesholm
(Associates Architects)
Anderson Bjornstad Kane Jacob Inc.
(Structural Engineers)
Consulting Design Inc.
(Mechanical Engineers)
The Berger Partnership
(Landscape)
Ellis-Don Construction Inc.
(General Constructor)

Location: University of Washington, Seattle, Washington, USA
Area: 10,000 sq. ft.
Construction Date: 1997
Photography: Farshid Assassi/Assassi Prod.
James Frederick Housel

A large patio is half-covered by an elevated platform that joins a bridge to separate part of the expansion of the original building (raised in 1929). The new intervention also adds on to the back of the old gallery to offer services and a lecture theater.

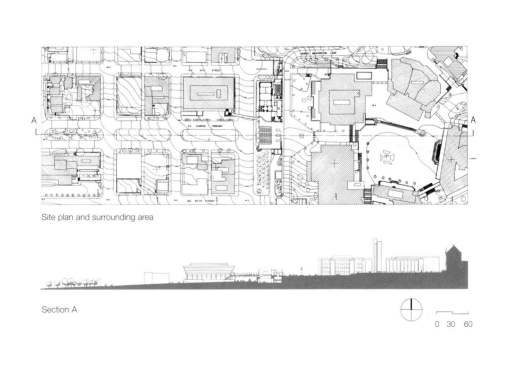

Site plan and surrounding area

Section A

0 30 60

Richard Long

Puget Sound Mud Circles
April 13 – August 31

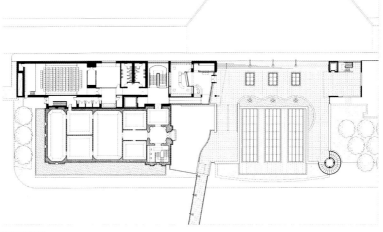

Second floor

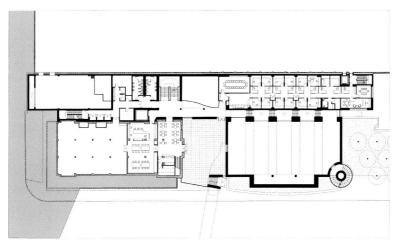

First floor

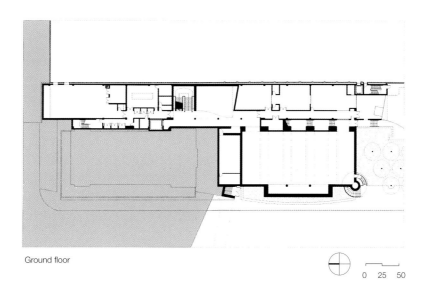

Ground floor

0   25   50

The new galleries rise up grandly, lighted from above and offering different options of subdivision to house a variety of exhibit types.

Visible from many parts of the city—particularly at night—the Levitt Center for University Advancement is an asymmetrical assemblage of geometric forms. The building is clad in Indiana limestone and articulates a hierarchical sequence of public gathering spaces and private work areas. The design solution responds to the client's request that the building's public assembly spaces be situated on the top floor, with views of the river and surrounding campus.

The five-story rotunda, whose exterior marks a visual and literal edge to the University of Iowa's Performing Arts Campus, anchors the complex and acts as its main public meeting and circulation space. This primary reception lobby integrates numerous works of art by faculty, students, and local artists. It is circled by a ceremonial stair and cantilevered bridges that create a promenade, leading visitors to the public assembly spaces located at the top of the building—typically a site for executive offices.

A double-height, circular boardroom with a terrace "sits" on the rotunda. This flexible space, capped by an inverted dome, is finished in cherry and features concentric, custom-designed conference tables. Divisible by acoustic panels into three separate spaces, the boardroom can be linked to the adjacent entertainment room, which implements sophisticated audiovisual systems.

The top floor of the building's bar element contains three major assembly halls, two roof terraces and a staff dining hall. The sculptural forms of these rooms distinguish their public functions from the three floors of administrative offices below and define a "cornice" to the arts campus.

Named for two of the university's most generous benefactors, the Levitt Center for University Advancement houses the University's Foundation, Alumni Association, and Division of Alumni Records and Services. It provides a central focus for all of the university's advancement-related activities: fund raising, alumni communications and outreach, student recruitment, public relations, economic development, and legislative liaison.

Collaborators: Brooks Borg & Skiles
Location: Iowa City, Iowa, USA
Area: 141,000 sq. ft.
Construction Date: 1998
Photography: Farshid Assassi, Richard Payne

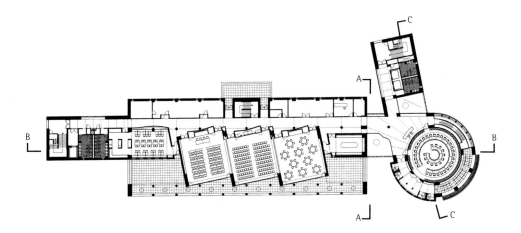

First floor

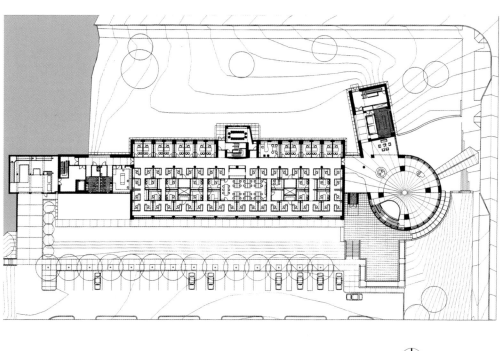

Ground floor

0 10 20

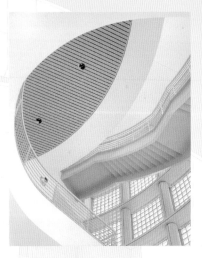

The triple-height cylindrical bay has an interior perimeter that includes a ceremonial staircase. The façade is of glass blocks, meaning bright natural light in the daytime hours and, from without, a lighthouse effect at night.

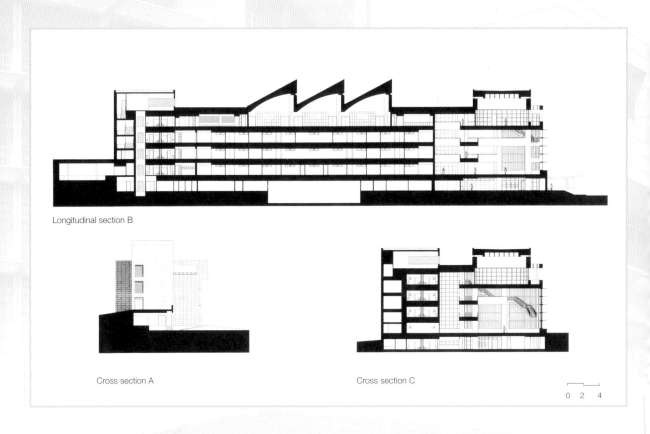

Longitudinal section B

Cross section A

Cross section C

0 2 4

This 15,000-square-foot addition houses the permanent exhibition galleries of the Busch-Reisinger Museum and its collection of German twentieth century paintings and decorative arts, as well as portions of the Fogg Museum's Fine Arts Library.

The major public spaces consist of the library reading room on the ground floor and the permanent collection galleries on the second floor. To the south are smaller scale spaces: on the ground floor, staff offices for the library; on the second floor, a temporary exhibition gallery; and on the third floor, the archival study area.

Its design responds to a number of unique site conditions, including the adjacent Carpenter Center for the Visual Arts, designed by Le Corbusier, an existing subterranean library by Jose Luis Sert and a required three-level connection to the Fogg Museum.

The building establishes a primary two-story facade facing the street and integrates a new exterior stair, plaza, and ramp at the library entry. Behind it, the building rises to three stories, complementing the Carpenter Center as a distinct yet related object perceived from all angles.

The fine arts library has a separate entrance from the gallery, thus resolving a security problem when the library and museum hours are different. With its high ceilings, tall windows, and visible reference stacks, the reading room conveys the stature associated with such spaces.

Existing streetscape and scale relationships had to be addressed, and constraints imposed by building above an existing underground library structure with limited load bearing capacity had to be accommodated.

The solution also resolves Le Corbusier's compelling site circulation idea. The Carpenter Center ramp, which was intended to provide a public mid-block walkway from Quincy Street to Prescott Street through the building, ended in the Fogg's rear yard without a connection to the sidewalk. The design extends the ramp onto a new plaza from which one can either enter the library or descend a new exterior stair to the street.

Collaborators: Severud Associates
(Structural Engineers)
Bard, Rao & Athanas
(MEP Engineers)
Jerry Kugler Associates
(Lighting Consultant)
Walsh Brothers Inc. (Contractor)
Location: Harvard University, Cambridge,
Massachusetts, USA
Area: 15,000 sq. ft.
Construction Date: 1991
Photography: Paul Warchol

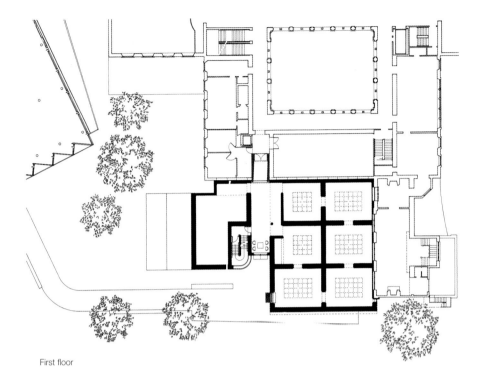

First floor

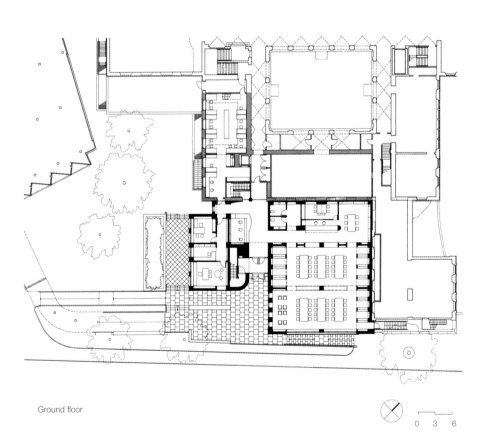

Ground floor

0   3   6

Axonometric perspective

The ramp designed by Le Corbusier extends to a new square from which the library or the street may be reached by a new external stairway.

On the first floor, the high bays destined for use as exhibition space for the Busch-Reisinger Museum's permanent collection are lighted from above.

The design used the zoning code currently in force in regard to emergency exits and dimensions. The project also had to solve problems related to the building's seating on a sub-grade foundation (the library), of limited load-bearing capacity.

Location Maps

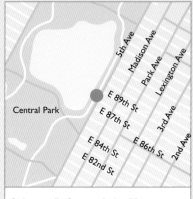

Solomon R. Guggenheim Museum

1071 Fifth Avenue, New York, USA

Lawrence Technological University

Southfield, Michigan, USA

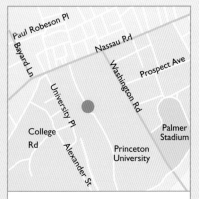

**James S. McDonnell Hall.
Princeton University**

Princeton, New Jersey, USA

**Morgan Stanley Dean Witter and Co.
World Headquarters**

1585 Broadway, New York, USA

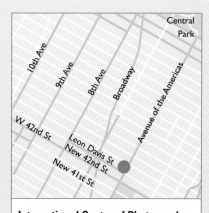

International Center of Photography

1133 Avenue of the Americas,
New York, USA

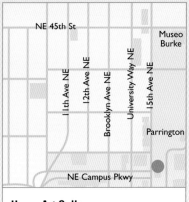

**Henry Art Gallery
University of Washington**

Seattle, Washington, USA

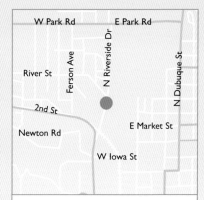

**Levitt Center.
University of Iowa**

180 North Riverside, Iowa City, USA

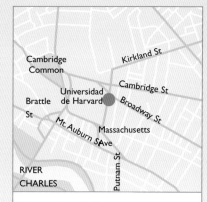

**Werner Otto Hall.
Harvard University**

32 Quincy Street, Cambridge,
Massachusetts, USA

Chronology of Works (2000-2004)

2000	The Graduate Center of the the City University of New York. New York, USA.
2000	The David Geffen Foundation Building. Beverly Hills, California, USA.
2000	50th Floor Restaurant of the Equitable Building. New York, USA.
2000	Pediatric Oncology Center of the New York Presbyterian Hospital, Columbia Presbyterian Campus, Herbert Irving Cancer Center. New York, USA.
2000	Sound View Plaza. New Rochelle, New York, USA.
2001	Casa Vecchia. Bel Air, California, USA.
2001	Einbender Apartment. New York, USA.
2001	FSU Library for Information Technology and Education (FLITE) of the Ferris State University. Big Rapids, Michigan, USA.
2001	International Center of Photography. New York, USA.
2001	Janklow Nesbit Offices. New York, USA.
2001	The Jewish Children's Museum. Brooklyn, New York, USA.
2001	University Technology and Learning Complex of the Lawrence Technological University. Southfield, Michigan, USA. In collaboraton with Neumann/Smith Architects.
2001	Greenberg Pavilion of the Louise Wells Cameron Art Museum. Wilmington, North Carolina, USA.
2001	Matlin Apartment. New York, USA.
2001	The Miranova Penthouse. Columbus, Ohio, USA.
2001	Comprehensive Cancer Center of the Montefiore Medical Center, Einstein Campus. Bronx, New York, USA.
2001	Comprehensive Cancer Center of the Montefiore Medical Center, Moses Campus. Bronx, New York, USA.
2001	Princeton Forrestal Center Office Building. Princeton, New Jersey, USA.
2001	Seinfeld Apartment. New York, USA.
2001	The Sackler Center for Arts Education of the Solomon R. Guggenheim Museum. New York, USA.
2002	Center for Information and Technology George E. Bello of the Bryant College. Smithfield, Rhode Island, USA.
2002	Maple Associates Ltd. Office Building. Beverly Hills, California, USA.
2003	Akron-Summit County Public Library. Akron, Ohio, USA. In collaboration with Richard Fleischman Architects.
2003	Burchfield-Penney Art Center. Buffalo, New York, USA.
2003	Middlebury College Library. Middlebury, Vermont, USA.
2003	Naismith Memorial Basketball Hall of Fame and Retail Complex. Springfield, Massachusetts, USA.
2003	U.S. Mission to the United Nations. New York, USA.
2003	Student Center of the University of Cincinnati. Cincinnati, Ohio, USA.
2004	Addition and renovation of the Allen County Public Library. Fort Wayne, Indiana, USA. In collaboration with MSKTD & Associates.
2004	Student Center and Academic Building for the New Jersey Institute of Technology. Newark, New Jersey, USA.
2004	Renovation and expansion of the New York Public Library, Mid-Manhattan Library. New York, USA. In collaboraton with Richard Fleischman Architects.